To Lisa and Cortland, who inspire me daily.
To the educators who inspired this book
and to the students who embrace it.

Endorsements

"John Jell tells a personal story about common sense action plans and real-world applications that will help prepare any student or young adult for a successful career. His ideas and experiences are excellent and provide solid advice."

—Dr. John A. Lammel, past president,
National Association of Secondary School Principals

"John Jell's book provides a wealth of knowledge and is a valuable tool in helping students transition from school to the workforce."

—Jean Buckley, president, Future Business Leaders of America

"This book is a wonderful tool for students beginning to explore career options—necessary at the high school level to prepare for work and further education. It is also a must read for counselors, advisors, as well as teachers. Employers will look forward to hiring such prepared young people."

—Ms. Deanna Hanson, chief executive officer, Linking Education and Economic Development

Contents

Acknowledgments

While I was in college, I began keeping notes in the hopes of writing a book on helping youth to better prepare for life after school. When I was promoted by the Coca-Cola Company from Canada to Los Angeles, I dug out my notes and began writing a book that I thought 1) today's students could use, 2) should be written in language they could understand, and 3) told the full story on preparing for life after school.

After writing my first draft, I sent copies out to many people in the business and education communities. These individuals validated that there was a need for my message, and to several I am forever indebted. My first book, *A Student's Guide to Success in the Real World: Method to the Madness,* was subsequently published in 1997.

First, I must thank Dr. John A. Lammel, currently a professor at the University of Nebraska. He is the former president and director of High School Services for the National Association of Secondary School Principals. His insight, wisdom, coaching, and support over many years have been a blessing.

I also want to thank Dr. Edward Miller and Ms. Jean Buckley, the former and current presidents of the Future Business Leaders of America. Their support for this project will never be forgotten, nor will the support of DECA executive director Dr. Edward Davis, who not only provided valuable feedback but also gave me the chance to launch my first book at DECA's annual convention. (DECA, for those of you who aren't familiar with it, is a worthwhile organization dedicated to enhancing the cocurricular education of students with interests in marketing, management, and entrepreneurship.)

Getting a book published is an arduous journey. I owe a debt of gratitude and appreciation to Dr. Thomas Koerner and Cindy Tursman, the editorial team at Scarecrow Education, who agreed with those who have endorsed this book that it needed to be in your hands.

I would be remiss if I also did not thank three individuals at my original publishing company, formerly Technomic (Lancaster, Pennsylvania): Dr. Joe Eckenrode, Susan Farmer, and Steve (You 'da man) Spangler.

Writing a book is one thing, but getting it reviewed and embraced is another. To the editors of the American Counseling Association, the American School Counseling Association, and the *School Library Journal*, who read my original book and gave me their highest ratings, I thank you! To those whose names you find on the back cover of this edition, I am humbled by your support!

To each person who embraced my message and invited me to speak, I thank you! To all educators, parents, and community and business leaders who support the cause of *From School to a Career*, your commitment has made a big difference!

After my first book was published, many educators dispensed great advice, most notably that a more condensed version was needed, with fewer statistics, focused on the core concepts, with better packaging, that could be better incorporated into vocational/technical programs and high school freshman curriculums. They suggested a new "general" version to complement the original book, which could become the "advanced" edition. To each of you who gave me this feedback, the book you are holding in your hands today is a direct result.

From my business life, there are too many individuals to recognize who have touched my life in a positive way (you know who you are); however, there are a few who deserve special mention. First, Mr. Ed Ray, the former head of Global Training for Coca-Cola—Ed taught me how to be a true public speaking professional and always lent an ear when I needed one. Second, I want to thank Jim Leishman, who created a position for me to be hired at Coca-Cola when I graduated.

On the Nestlé side, there are four individuals I want to give recognition to. First, to Pat Cole, who had the confidence to hire me and give me the corporate challenge of a lifetime. Second, to Phil Ray. I have met many human resource professionals in my life, but Phil is first class all the way! Third, Jess Nepstad, who gave me an ear or a pat on the back, and always when I needed one. Last, but certainly not least, I want to thank Rita Henderson, who got me involved in educational initiatives.

Finally, last, but certainly not least, words cannot express my gratitude to the two biggest loves of my life: my wife and my daughter. From staying up late at night writing, through the ups and downs of trying to get published, to using most of my vacation time to speak at conferences, my wife's patience and unwavering support has made your reading this today possible. I love you, babe!

My daughter is also a tremendous source of inspiration. Her wit, smile, and love help to complete every day. When I speak at conferences, I always share a not-new, but ever-so-inspiring quote with educators that was once shared with me. It goes something like this: "A hundred years from now, it will not matter the sort of house I lived in, what my bank account was, or the car I drove, but the world may be different because I was important in the life of a child."

It is for my daughter, her classmates, today's students, and for future generations that I continue to preach my message on properly preparing for life after school. My work will be done when there is no student left who cannot find a great career opportunity immediately upon graduating. Until then, to the educators who use this book in their schools, I thank you for your support! To the students who read it, I hope you will be able to apply my experiences and coaching to build a competitive advantage come graduation day. I wish each and every one of you the best for success. To parents, I hope this book helps fill a developmental void that has existed for years. To the business community, I can only hope my efforts will help save you millions in training and turnover costs.

If you wish to contact me regarding a speaking engagement or drop me a line, you can find my particulars in the about the author section. All the best!

Introduction

Okay . . . where do we want to start? First, let me ask you a question. When you graduate from school, would you like to make at least $40,000 per year, if not more, and have great career opportunities ahead of you with an employer you like working for? Let me guess . . . you said "yes."

Today is your lucky day! You are about to read a book that will help you make a successful transition from school to a career.

When I was in school, if my teachers gave me a textbook, I automatically did not want to read it. To me, many textbooks were very boring. Lots of big words and no pictures. That's why I wrote this book differently. It outlines many things you need to know that school has not yet taught you. A few real-life stories and examples, tied in with a few pictures, will speed you to the end of the book before you know it!

Better yet, I hope you will remember everything I share with you and do all of the exercises so that, come graduation day, you will have your choice of great career opportunities. When someone asks you twenty years from now what was the most important book you ever read, I can only hope that you remember this one.

Life is all about choices! You can make smart choices or poor choices. Before I get into telling you everything you need to know to focus and make smart choices regarding your future, I want to give you a little snapshot about my background and how I got to be where I am today. If I could have my choice of rewarding career opportunities upon graduation, then so can you!

I remember the day my life changed like it was yesterday. It was Friday, November 20, several years ago. It was a gloomy, cloudy day. I was six years old, my sister was eight, and we were walking home from school. When we were about one hundred yards from our driveway (more like a laneway—we lived on the outskirts of town), we saw a white station wagon taxi speed toward our house. My sister and I looked at each other, then ran home to see why the taxi was there. When we got home, we found out why. There was our mom, standing on the doorstep crying, with three garbage bags full of clothes. All she said was, "Get in the taxi, we are leaving."

I had never heard of the word *divorce* before that day, but I sure learned fast what it was all about. When I was six, divorce was very rare, unlike today, where as many as one in three children live in a single-parent family. Some divorces are friendly; many are not. The latter was true in my family's case. The custody battle was very bitter, and in the end, my dad ended up with my sister and me. How he did that (and why my mom left) is a topic in another book of mine, but it is safe to say that my childhood became more complicated because of this. I heard a statistic that in the year my parents split up, 99.9 percent of the custody cases went to the mother. Well, now you know why it wasn't 100 percent.

Growing up was not a lot of fun. By the time I turned seventeen, within my immediate family (mother, father, sister), I had to deal with things such as mental and physical abuse, alcoholism, an attempted suicide by drug overdose, and manic depression—and that is only scratching the surface. It was at this time that I said to myself, "Enough of this! I want to take control of my life!" And take control I did. (I will walk you through how you can too.)

One of my biggest goals in life, then, was to have a strong family: to be a great husband and great father and provide my family with all of the things I never had growing up. I knew I wanted to get into the business world and move up so that I could make enough money to comfortably provide for my family, and to do that, I knew I would have to go to college. But then life threw me another curve ball.

Like cars are to Detroit, big combines for harvesting crops and agricultural equipment were to my hometown of Brantford. Imagine what it would be like if they stopped building cars in Detroit and the impact that would have on the city, the loss of jobs. Well, that is what happened in my hometown. The combine industry packed up and moved out, or went bankrupt. My dad had worked on the factory floor for over twenty-nine years and was close to retirement when he lost his job. My mom was on a disability pension and could not work. I found myself in the position that if I wanted to go to college, I was going to have to pay for it myself, which I did.

I started working when I was twelve with a paper route and stayed employed continuously throughout high school and college. During high school, I worked in several different industries, which helped me focus on a desired career area (we'll discuss this later). During four years of college, I usually held one job during school and at least two jobs during the summer, plus a part-time painting business. I never went away in the summer, at Christmas, or spring break, because every day I did not work cost me $50–$75 that I really needed (and there are thousands of other kids who have done the same).

Working hard in my part-time and summer jobs helped me to get the funds I needed to pay for college and helped me focus on a career in sales and marketing when I got to college. Although I was a good student through elementary and high school, in college my grades started to slide, because I disliked many of my courses. I was frustrated because I did not think I was learning everything I needed to be successful once I got into the "Real World." I took it upon myself to learn what I thought was missing in books and in the classroom (things I will share with you) by getting involved in campus and community activities and by knocking on employers' doors if no jobs existed. I needed to graduate, but I also needed relevant experience in my desired field, and if the opportunities did not come to me, I tried to create my own.

When it came to work experience, although I got my share of doors slammed in my face, opportunities did surface. Not only did I get relevant work experience (we'll discuss how important this is), I was also able to learn valuable skills employers are looking for—skills that cannot be learned from books, skills you can only learn from life.

In college, I knew there were other students who were going to graduate at the same time I did and compete for the same opportunities I wanted. At the back of this book, you will find my graduating resumé. When I graduated, I had my choice of not one but two jobs created for me by The Coca-Cola Company, plus two job offers from other big-name companies. At that time, Coca-Cola was the hottest company on the planet and did not recruit from college campuses in my neck of the woods; they usually waited to hire people who had three to five years of experience gained at another company's expense. Yet here was a kid from a dysfunctional, single-parent family, from a depressed town, who got in. How? I networked to meet people from Coca-Cola and worked hard over four years to build a resumé that, come graduation day, gave me a competitive advantage over every other graduating student from across the country.

Because of the skills I was able to develop during my years in high school and college, in just over six years I went from an entry-level sales position in Canada to rebuilding a $350 million segment of Coca-Cola's business in the United States. As I moved up the ladder, I was usually the youngest person in the country at that level of management. Today, I still remain the only person promoted from Canadian bottling operations to the parent company in the United States.

After many good years with Coca-Cola, the world's #1 beverage company, a change in company culture forced me to make a choice: stay and feel unchallenged or get out of my comfort zone and test my skill set in other industries. I opted for the latter. I was rewarded with many challenges and chances to grow professionally that would not have happened had I stayed at Coca-Cola at that time. Because I was able to continue to build my skill set, I subsequently worked my way into another great company, one that happens to be the world's #1 food company, Nestlé.

In this book, I will walk you through what you need to do to prepare for the working world beyond school. I wrote this book to (1) let you learn the "easy" way what my friends and I had to learn the hard way, and (2) dispel the myths still around, like "Go to school, get good grades, get a degree, and the world will be at your feet."

Some of you may be asking yourself right now, "What do you mean it's a myth?!" Don't panic! Graduating is very important, but so are many other things that have never really been discussed at home or in classrooms. I thought I would take the guesswork out and give you the chance to start thinking and preparing for your future *now* so you won't be one of those students who graduates and says, "Hey, I have my diploma, I have racked up a bunch of student loans, but I cannot find a job."

Many of the exercises in this book can help you whenever you get to a fork in the road of life. Making the transition successfully from school to the workforce will be one of the first big forks you will have to deal with. Having your choice of opportunities is really not that hard if you become focused on what you really want to do and if you are not afraid of applying yourself. Trust me on this . . . if I can do it, so can you!

1

What Do You Want to Do in the Future?

Where do we start as it relates to your future?

Before we look at the future, let's look at some things that have changed over the years, and some that have not changed. With respect to things that have changed, there are more children than ever living in single-parent families. Many children are also being raised at or below the poverty line. Tuition rates have only gone up at colleges. Guns, AIDS, and violence in our schools have also had a big impact. The price of housing has gone up dramatically, and many families have both parents working just to pay the bills.

As the future relates to things that have not changed, there is only one factor: Change remains constant! The economy goes through cycles. There are periods of prosperity and periods of recession. There are times when the labor market is great and times when unemployment is high. The job market is extremely competitive. For people already in the workforce, those who are focused, prepared, and apply themselves will get through the good times and the bad. They have learned to adapt to change and make the best of any situation. As it relates to those about to enter the workforce, there are countless great opportunities for graduating students every year, regardless of prosperity or recession. The only difference today versus twenty-five years ago is that the employers who provide the best opportunities have a lot more talent to choose from.

If you want to be successful—whether you are a welder, mechanic, accountant, sales person, nurse, whatever—the best opportunities go to the best graduating students. Remember, come graduation time, you are not only competing with others who graduate from your school but competing with individuals from other schools in your city, your state, and from every other state across the country.

And what separates the "best" from the "rest"? Usually, the "best" have focused on a field they really liked while in high school, went to college to learn more about it, and gained experience outside of the classroom relevant to their desired field. The "rest" struggle well into their twenties, and sometimes thirties, because they still have not figured out what they want to do with the rest of their lives. The "best" also had the ability to plan, set, and achieve their goals. (We'll discuss goals a little later on.)

REALITY CHECK QUESTIONS

But how do you focus on your future? Where do you start so you can properly channel your energy and time? Let's start with three questions I have used throughout my life. I call them "reality check questions." They are simply:

1. Where am I now?
2. Where do I want to go?
3. How am I going to get there?

Ask yourself these three questions right now.

The first question is easy, right? You probably are at home or at school in your town or city reading this book, but I'll bet many of you cannot answer #2, and if you cannot answer #2, there is absolutely no way you can answer #3.

Question #2 is the critical question, because knowing where you want to go requires setting some goals, and if you cannot get focused on clear goals, how are you going to put in place an action plan to achieve them?

WHERE DO YOU SEE YOURSELF IN TWENTY-FIVE YEARS?

To help you answer question #2, let me ask you another question, and this time I want you to look at the pyramid on the next page. The question is, "Where do you want to see yourself in twenty-five years?"

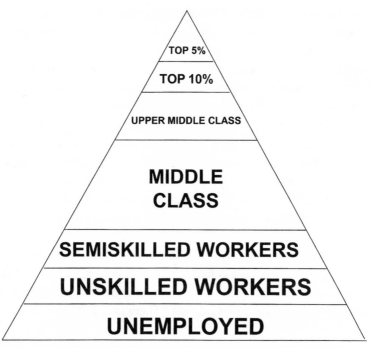

Figure 1.1. Career/Job Pyramid. Reprinted by permission of Nightingale-Conant Corporation.

We know that the average person today lives to be around seventy-five years old. We all have twenty-four hours in a day, seven days in a week, and 365 days in a year. Some people will stay at the bottom of the pyramid their whole life while others, like Bill Gates of Microsoft and Michael Dell of Dell Computer, reached the very top as multibillionaires before they turned thirty-five!

Everyone has to realistically determine where they want to be on this pyramid for themselves and then take the steps necessary to try to get where they want to go (we'll discuss this in great detail). Some people will define their success by how much money they have, how big their homes are, and how big their cars are. For others, success may be defined by making the most of every day and helping others. Each of us defines success differently. You need to define for yourself what success is. One comment, though: If you can see a big house, big cars, and lots of expensive toys in your future and don't win the lottery or get a big inheritance, you will have to be prepared to work hard (like everyone else before you) to make the big bucks.

Going from school to the workforce is a major transition in life. It does not hurt to begin thinking about it now and try to picture where you want to be in a few years to help answer the reality check questions. And what happens down the road when you are working and decide you want to do something different, like change employers because you have a lousy boss, or change your career because you are bored?

As discussed earlier in this book, life is all about choices. Later in the book, I will walk you through some exercises that will help you get through the reality check questions whenever you get to a fork in the road, because there are many out there. The exercises have helped me many times since I graduated to choose which road to take. One of the forks you will be at shortly is deciding whether you want a job or a career.

Now, go back to the pyramid. On the bottom half, most of the categories are job related, whereas most of the categories on the top half are career related. There is a transition in the middle between the two. Is there a difference between a job and a career? There sure is!

JOBS VERSUS CAREERS

As defined by Webster's dictionary, a job is "a specific duty, role, or function . . . a regular remunerative position." Basically, it means you get an hourly rate to do the same thing over and over every day. A career is "a field for or pursuit of consecutive progressive achievement." Careers tend to be salaried (no time-and-a-half overtime pay) and involve a person going through a series of positions. Look at the chart on the next page. It will clearly show you the difference between a job and a career. It involves someone I met at a restaurant chain I used to work for.

This person started off in high school washing dishes and worked her way to chef. She worked full-time in summer and part-time through college for this chain as both a chef and a relief assistant manager. After graduating, she was hired as manager to run a location that was struggling. Because she did well in this position, she was promoted to district manager to improve results for a group of stores. History repeated itself, and this person then went on to become the regional manager and ultimately a vice president.

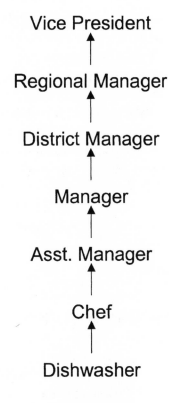

Figure 1.2.   Job/Career Comparison

Guess what? This same story has happened in many different industries. I know a student from my high school who loved working on cars, went to community college to learn how to use all of the latest diagnostic equipment, started working for a garage, and ultimately opened his own shop. Today, he makes more money every year than most corporate executives I know.

As you can see, there is a difference between a job and a career. When we started this book, most of you said "yes" to making at least $40,000 per year and to great career opportunities ahead of you upon graduating. Most students I have met want the opportunities and, even more, the "big bucks!" To get those opportunities, you have to be able to honestly answer the reality check questions and also apply yourself. But what are the things employers look for that provide these opportunities?

CHAPTER SUMMARY

- The transition from school to the workforce is a major transition in life.
- The best employment opportunities will go to the best-prepared students.
- Each person has to define success for himself or herself, as success is not solely defined by how much money you have.
- The reality check questions are important throughout your entire life. Answering them can help you when you get to forks in the road of life.
- A job is a specific duty, role, or function.
- A career is progressive achievement by holding a variety of positions.

APPLICATION

- Which do you think is better: a job or a career? Why?
- Can you answer the three reality check questions:
  - Where am I now?
  - Where do I want to go?
  - How am I going to get there?

If not, can you think of two or three career areas that may be of interest to you in the future? Why are you interested in these areas? (Please keep your notes, as I will be asking you to come back to this later.)

- Think about the example of the dishwasher who became a vice president. Can you think of your own example of someone who has had a job and someone who has had a career? For the person who had the career, can you trace how he or she arrived where he or she is today?
- Why do the best employment opportunities go to the best-prepared students?

2

What Employers Are Looking For

In today's world, employers have a lot of talent to choose from. Recent data shows that many young workers today will make at least five job changes in their productive years, so employers want to get the most out of their investment in training and development. Most employers prefer graduating students that can bring as many of the following to the table:

- A postsecondary degree or diploma
- Relevant work experience
- Time management skills
- Networking skills
- People management, teamwork, and leadership skills
- Strong verbal and written communication skills
- The initiative to set and achieve goals as well as complete tasks.

I'll discuss each point separately and briefly explain why each is important. First, why a degree or diploma?

In today's world, regardless of your desired field, advanced learning beyond high school is available from a technical school, career college, community college, or a university. Given the competition for the highest paying opportunities, a degree or diploma in a related subject to your desired career is even better. It shows employers you took the time and invested the dollars to learn things that they will not have to spend money to teach you.

Now, I have to make a comment. When I was in college studying business, an instructor told me, "When you get out of here, at best, you might use 20 percent of what you learned in books on a daily basis." I thought to myself, "Wow. . . . I'm spending all of this money and I won't use most of this. . . . What is the other 80 percent I need to know?" Look at the bullet points at the beginning of this chapter listing all of the other things noted after the degree/diploma. (Note: The 20 percent statistic above is what my instructor said regarding my desired career in sales and marketing. That does not mean it will apply to whatever career you choose.)

RELEVANT WORK EXPERIENCE

Relevant work experience is very important to prospective full-time employers. Relevant means your experience is related to your desired career area. If the area you like is accounting, you will have had summer or part-time jobs (or even volunteered time) doing accounting. If it is auto body, you will have worked at an auto body shop. Let me drive home a point by sharing two examples with you. The first is from a story I once read in the newspaper; the second is related to someone I knew.

In the newspaper article, a recent college graduate was upset because he did not get an interview for a $40,000/year entry-level marketing position. The reporter asked the student, "What were the requirements?" The student replied, "A degree and work experience." The reporter then asked, "Why are you upset?" The student replied, "I have a degree and work experience and should have had an interview." The reporter then asked, "What is your degree in and what work experience do you have?" The student replied, "I have a degree in sociology, I was a lifeguard for two summers, and I did some filing work for a lawyer another summer. See . . . I have a degree and work experience."

Can you tell me why this person did not get an interview? If you said their degree and work experience were not relevant to the marketing position, you are correct! What are the chances that someone else across the country with a degree or diploma in business, with a marketing major, and possibly some experience in sales and marketing, also applied?

Here is a second scenario. I was speaking to a fellow passenger on an airplane one day who had a son, whom we will call Bob. Bob wanted to be an electrician. A very good friend of theirs owned an electrical contracting company, and Bob knew that the electricians there got paid $25/hour. He asked his mom to set him up with a job, because he wanted to make those dollars. However, when he got the job offer, he was very upset because their family friend was only willing to pay him minimum wage. How could a family friend only pay him minimum wage when all of the other guys were making $25? He thought he should be making that too. Can you guess why he was not offered $25/hour?

Well, first, as the owner of the electrical company was a family friend, he did offer a job to Bob, which was nice of him to do. He also asked him two questions: "How much do you know about being an electrician?" Bob's answer was "nothing." Then the owner asked the second question: "If you know nothing about being an electrician, why should I pay you $25/hour when I will have to train you? I can hire someone who just graduated from the local community college electrical program and they will be able to do all the work I need right away." Bob had no answer this time; he was speechless.

In this case, Bob had no relevant diploma and no relevant experience, yet his expectation was that he could make big bucks anyway. In the end, Bob took the job at minimum wage, went to the local community college to study electrical engineering, eventually turned his minimum wage job into an apprenticeship, and when he graduated, guess what? . . . He was making $25/hour.

In today's world, relevant experience and completing a postsecondary education are things employers are looking for. There are too many students who have graduated ahead of you who did not understand this. (They had better watch out for you when you start working, because you know better.) As there are very few positions and jobs that do not involve working with people and managing some level of stress, employers must hire graduates who also bring critical skills.

CRITICAL SKILLS

As we just discussed, relevant studies and experience for your desired career will help you to secure the best opportunities. However, there are many critical skills that employers also value and that you must learn to be successful once you get out of school. There are "hard" skills and "soft" skills. Hard skills relate to your functional and technical expertise, like working on a computer, framing a house, preparing a meal, or fixing a car. Soft skills relate to your interpersonal and organizational skills. Hard skills can often be learned from courses in school. Soft skills are often learned from life. I want to focus on the key soft skills employers are looking for and give a brief explanation why each is important:

- *Time management*—being able to juggle ten projects at any given moment while dealing with fire drills and questions from customers, bosses, and coworkers is tough. Bosses also usually do not give extensions, like some teachers do for essays and projects. Procrastination in the working world can kill your chances for a great career. Employers want individuals who complete tasks on time!
- *Networking*—Have you ever heard the saying "It's not what you know, it's who you know"? Networking involves getting to know people who can help you achieve goals. These folks keep in touch with people regularly, not just when they need something. Doors open when other people like you and want to help you, often because you like them and want to help them too. Like a spider that spins its web, people who can network spin their own too. Asking someone to set you up on a date with his or her friend, whom you have a crush on, is a good example of networking. Another example: Had I not kept in touch with the people I met from Coca-Cola when I was in college, I can guarantee you I never would have been hired upon graduating.
- *People management, teamwork, and leadership skills*—Whether you want to own your own business or work your way up the ladder, dealing with people will be vital to your success. Every person has different needs, goals, and talents. Being able to manage the expectations and earn the respect of those above you and below you can make or break your success. So too will learning the art of "asking" versus "telling." For example, which approach do you like better when your mom wants you to clean up your room—first, she asks, "Please clean up your room," and after you did, she said "Thank you," or second, she yells and tells you, "Clean up your room now!" and never says anything after you did. Likely the first (unless she po-

litely asked you a couple of times before). There is only one way to get respect from your team and peers . . . you earn it!

- *Strong verbal and written communication skills*—Whether writing a letter or standing up and giving a presentation, being concise and to the point is a very important skill. Most bosses don't want to read essays. You have to get everything onto one page or give them the "Cliff Notes" version . . . everything they need to know in ninety seconds or less. (Note: Public speaking is a very important skill. Take every chance to refine your skills here. Every time you get up in front of a group, the next time becomes that much easier.)

GOALS

Earlier, I discussed setting goals, like answering reality check question #2: Where do I want to go? As defined by Webster's dictionary, a goal is "the end toward which effort is directed." Goals can be short term, like losing ten pounds in the next three months, or long term, like landing a great career opportunity when you graduate. As learning is a never-ending process, so too is goal setting. Set your sights on something, work hard to achieve it, and once you do, set your sights on something else worthy of your time and efforts.

Employers really like people who can set and achieve goals. Today, they can be very picky, because they lose millions of dollars every year training people who end up quitting. They want people who can do a great job, are motivated, can take initiative, and who are not afraid to apply themselves and take some chances to overcome a challenge. These people can see what needs to be done and then do it, without having to be told as well. As was once told to me, "There are three types of people in this world. There are those who make things happen, those who watch what happens, and those who wonder what happened."

Whenever you start a new job, you have to watch what happens and learn. Employers understand this, but after a "ramp-up" period, they expect you to make things happen. Those who always wonder "what happened" usually find themselves in the unemployment line, because employers want people who will work, not people who want to get paid to show up and do nothing after they arrive except gossip or sit around.

To illustrate this, let's pretend you own your own home and are putting in a pool. The concrete just dried, yet there is a big pile of dirt on your lawn that has to be shoveled into the hole around the pool because the contractor had to dig a little extra out. You call two neighborhood kids and advise them to shovel the dirt as you have to run some errands. You tell them the shovel and wheelbarrow will be in the garage. They like the fact that you will pay $10 an hour.

The first shows up, sees the garage door closed, sees your car gone, and sits and waits for you. After one hour, he goes home. The second one shows up, sees the garage door closed, knocks on the door and asks your spouse to open the door so he can get the wheelbarrow and shovel. He then goes out back, sees the pile of dirt, fills the hole, and then rakes all around to make certain the dirt was spread evenly. He does this in two hours. You get home and pay him $20 before he leaves.

Later in the day, the first person shows up and asks to be paid $10 for the time spent because he showed up to do the work but could not get the tools needed. Would you pay him? I would not have (although I would have not only paid the second the $10 per hour, but also given him a $10 tip for saving me having to do the raking).

I have met some students over the years who say, "Why should I take initiative and do something I wasn't told to do? . . . Nobody will see what I did and I won't get any credit." Trust me on this one . . . people really do notice. Learn how to take initiative now! It is one skill that will pay huge dividends over the years. Another thing that will pay big dividends is balancing your education between academic studies and the critical skills highlighted in this chapter relevant to your desired field.

CHAPTER SUMMARY

- Employers today want people who complete a postsecondary education.
- Employers today want people who have relevant work experience as well as time, stress, leadership, and people-management skills, and the ability to set and achieve goals.
- Hard skills relate to functional and technical skills.

- Soft skills relate to interpersonal and organizational skills.
- Networking is a very important skill. Get to know, and stay in touch with, people who may be able to help you. You never know when they will be able to open a door for you.
- Goals are the ends to which effort is directed.
- Goals can be short term or long term.
- Employers really like people who can set and achieve goals.
- Taking initiative without being told to do something is another very important skill employers like.

APPLICATION

- On a scale of 1 to 10, how would you rate yourself on the following?

  - Time-management skills   _____
  - People-management skills   _____
  - Leadership skills   _____
  - Verbal communication skills   _____
  - Written communication skills   _____
  - Ability to set and achieve goals   _____
  - Ability to take initiative   _____
  - Ability to complete assigned tasks on time   _____

- Think about goals for a minute. Have you ever set one? What was the goal? Did you achieve it? What led you to achieve, or not achieve, your goal?
- Which goals do you prefer: ones you set for yourself or those that others set for you? Why?
- Set one short-term goal to accomplish within the next six months. A good start would be one of the areas you may have scored yourself low in the first question. What do you wish to do by when?
- Set one new goal for yourself regarding your future career plans. How might you be able to challenge yourself to achieve that goal by listing three specific activities? If you accomplish that goal, what is the next goal that might follow?

- Think of one situation where networking has helped you. What was it? What were you trying to accomplish?
- Can you think of a situation in the future where networking might be able to help you? What steps will you take moving forward from today?

3

The Importance of Balancing Formal and Informal Learning

FORMAL VERSUS INFORMAL LEARNING

In chapter 2, we discussed what employers are looking for and the need to not only complete a postsecondary education but also build relevant skills and experience. I can summarize the question of how to properly prepare for life after school with a simple picture, which is illustrated below.

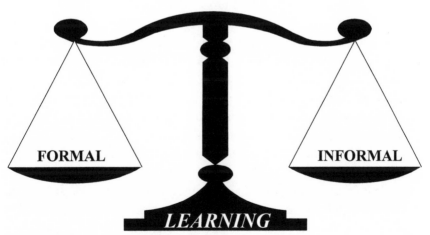

Figure 3.1.   Formal versus Informal Learning

It requires balancing your formal and informal learning. Formal learning is what you learn in school primarily from reading books, doing assignments and experiments, and writing tests. Informal learning is what you learn primarily from life, by being exposed to different people and situations and applying what you may have learned in the formal learning process.

To illustrate the importance of both formal and informal learning, let me walk you through my journey into Coca-Cola and describe how important both were to me.

I was usually a straight-A student in grade school and high school. I was lucky in that I could cram for exams well, but within fifteen minutes of finishing the test I had completely forgotten everything I had learned. When I got to college, my study habits were not as good as those of many friends of mine, who had worked hard to get Bs in high school. As I watched their grades go up, mine went in another direction, because I disliked many of my courses. However, I did much better than many other students. In my freshman year, there were almost five hundred students. Come graduation day, there were just over two hundred . . . about a 40 percent graduation rate (only two of every five students who started finished the program in four years).

While in college, an instructor of mine in my sophomore year encouraged us to get involved in clubs and committees, stating that many employers looked for people with a broad background and good skills, not just the diploma. I took his words to heart and became involved in campus and community affairs. I got hooked, because I was developing all of the critical soft skills I discussed in the last chapter. In my senior year, I was a chairman, vice chairman, president, and senator, and I sat on eight committees. Not only did I have a blast, I was able to network and meet great people from well-known companies, and the best part was that my grades improved as I became more motivated.

Academically, I did not graduate at the top of the class, but at least I graduated from college, unlike 60 percent of my freshman class. However, the investment in time I made to develop relevant skills and experience while in school got me into the world's #1 company at the time. My starting salary, benefits, and the career opportunities that lay ahead of me actually moved me to the top 1 percent of my class—thus the significance and value of a background of multiple experiences.

HOW MUCH OF WHAT WE LEARN DO WE RETAIN?

To examine the importance of formal and informal learning in closer detail, look at figure 3.2. What do you see? Can you distinguish how informal learning can help reinforce formal learning?

Reading something is a form of formal learning. If we only read something, like a chapter of this book, you will likely be able to remember only 10 percent. If you hear some of the things discussed, your retention will improve. If you get a chance to "say and do" what you read, your retention can be as high as 90 percent (that is why there are exercises at the end of every chapter in this book).

Let's look at an example of how formal and informal learning work. Two students are taking courses in accounting. Both read the same textbooks and have the same grades. One finds a part-time accounting job helping a local business; the other finds a part-time job at the local movie theater taking tickets. The one who got the accounting job is applying what she learned in the books, enhancing her learning retention. The

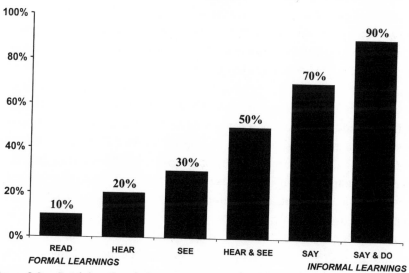

Figure 3.2. Retaining Knowledge. *Source* Robert Pike: Creative Training Techniques Handbook.

movie ticket taker is not. Whom do you think would be more attractive to a full-time employer who wants to hire an accountant?

Therein lies the importance of formal and informal learning. If you have a chance to read something and then apply it, your retention goes through the roof, versus if you did not "do" it. I want to take a moment right now to talk about something we discussed before: applying yourself. Knowing how to go from "read," "hear," or "see" to "do" will make transition from school to the workforce, and ultimately success, a much easier process.

APPLYING YOURSELF

When I talk to teachers and counselors at conferences, they always tell me they have only two types of students: those who apply themselves and those who do not. When I ask them what percentage belongs to each group, many have told me the same numbers: 20 percent are motivated, 80 percent are not very motivated and tend to "just show up." (It is funny, but many bosses will tell you the same numbers regarding their employees.)

Now, I want to be fair. Most unmotivated people, including myself on many occasions during my life, are not lazy out of habit. We tend to be lazy when we are uninterested or bored with what is going on around us. The challenge, then, is to find something that gets our adrenaline rushing (hold this thought regarding your future career plans for exercises we will go through in chapter 6).

Although I had good grades in high school, I would not have called myself very motivated. Lucky for me, I did well in required courses like history, math, and English. Some friends of mine did well in technical courses but not in history, math, or English. In my elective classes, I avoided technical courses because they would have pulled my grades down. I was a walking hazard around any machine or a hammer. After school, we usually just hung out.

Eventually, I attended a university to study business, and my friends went to a regional community college to strengthen their technical knowledge related to trades they enjoyed. They earned apprenticeships afterward, and, trust me on this, a couple of them make more money per year than several corporate executives I know. (They were great at what they did, eventually opened their own shops, and have not looked back for one minute.)

During my college years, the motivation tables turned for me, compared to high school, because the stakes were much higher. I was working hard to pay for my education, and I knew I could do well in the business world, but my grades were sliding. In order for me to get into a great organization and fulfill my dream of providing for my family at the level that I wanted, I had to:

1. Graduate . . . I could not flunk out.
2. Build a competitive advantage to get the opportunities I wanted to compete against everyone else who was going to graduate and compete for the same opportunities.

Applying yourself to balancing your formal and informal learning will lead you to different choices and opportunities. They can be summarized in figure 3.3 on the next page.

Let's walk through the chart. First, look to the left. If you get good grades and put some effort into building relevant skills and experience in your desired field, you will have good choices and optimize your opportunities. If you work *really* hard, have *really* good grades, and have a lot of relevant experience and skills for your desired career area, you will get better choices and maximize your opportunities. You could be the one getting a high-paying position with a great employer!

If you don't apply yourself toward your academics or skill-set building— or even worse, have no clue what your desired field is—you will have poor or bad choices. In both cases, you will end up with opportunities lost. You may also wind up like millions of twenty-something college graduates who have entered the workforce ahead of you, drifting aimlessly from one job to the next until they can figure out a career area that interests them.

A question to you right now: How can you apply yourself if you don't know exactly where to channel your time and energy? Well, I'll take you through some very important topics and exercises in the next couple of chapters to help you better understand the role of academics and experience, as well as give you some easy exercises so you can start getting focused today!

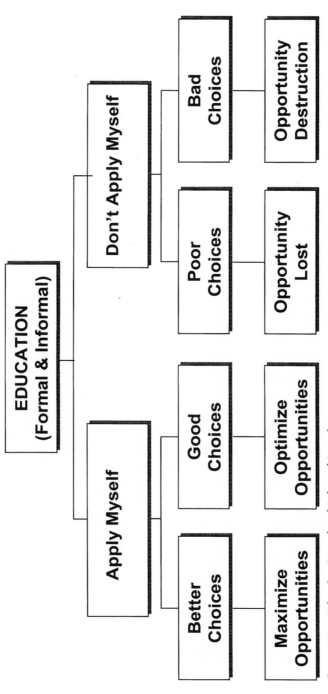

Figure 3.3. Balancing Formal and Informal Learning

CHAPTER SUMMARY

- Formal learning is what we learn from academic studies while in school.
- Informal learning is what we learn from life and the experiences of interacting with other people.
- To prepare for securing the best career opportunities, you must balance your formal and informal learning.
- Learning retention is much higher if you not only read something but also have a chance to apply it.
- Those students who apply themselves in balancing their formal and informal learning will have better opportunities than those who do not.

APPLICATION

- Which is more important to your future: formal learning or informal learning? Why?
- List three things you have learned from formal learning and three things from informal learning. How have they helped to shape who you are?
- In the example of two accounting students in this chapter, why would the student who got a part-time job doing books for a local business be more attractive to a prospective accounting employer than the one who got a job taking tickets at the movie theater?
- Go back to the question in chapter 2 about a long-term career goal that you have set. How could you use formal *and* informal learning to help you get there?

4

The Role of Degrees, Grades, and Experience Come Graduation

Come graduation day, as we discussed already, employers will have their pick from a new crop of ex-students entering the workforce, not only from your city but from across your state, from across the country, and maybe from around the world. They will be looking for those individuals who balanced their formal and informal learning, and who developed relevant skills and experience.

Also recall the three reality check questions we discussed. Do you remember them? In case you cannot, here they are again:

1. Where am I now?
2. Where do I want to go?
3. How am I going to get there?

Those who can get focused on a career area that excites them while in high school are so far ahead of those who cannot. Why? Because they will be able to study a field that interests them and develop their work-relevant experience and skill set. They will have a definite competitive advantage over those who chose to do other things, such as party, play on the Internet, play video games, watch TV, or drift from one job to the next.

GRADUATION RATING SCALE

When it comes time to graduate, employers will want to pay the best dollars to the best people. In writing this book, I worked with many educators and business people, and I asked them one question: "If you were to rate recent graduates on a scale of 100 points, how would you do it?" Their answers looked like this:

Graduating with a postsecondary degree/diploma	40
Grade point average	10
Relevant experience and skill set	<u>50</u>
	100

Remember the picture showing the balance needed between formal and informal learning? What do you see here? If you said, "Fifty points for formal learning (graduating, GPA), and fifty points for informal learning (experience, skills)," you are right!

As I indicated earlier in the book, only 40 percent of my freshman class graduated with a degree in four years. I have also read statistics that show less than one out of three people who start school in kindergarten will graduate with a postsecondary degree or diploma. That is why 40 points are given to just graduating . . . so many students today will not get that far (don't be one of them).

When it comes to grades, many parents and educators will tell you that grades are all that matter. However, while they are very important to fields like accounting, finance, medicine, and engineering, as we have discussed, they are not the *only* factor for most jobs and career opportunities. (I know a lot of people in management positions who were history and sociology graduates who got hired by big-name banks.) When it comes to your grades, take your grade point average and translate that into a number on a scale of ten (for example, a 3.2 grade point average is equivalent to 8).

Then look at the following five skill-set areas. Each one is worth ten points. The better your level of development, the more points you will get, resulting in a number on a scale of fifty.

Time management skills
People-management/leadership skills

Verbal communication skills
Written communication skills
Relevant work experience.

To better illustrate how this rating scale works, let's look at two students competing for the $40,000 marketing job we discussed in chapter 2. The first student had a 4.0 GPA, the second had a 2.0 GPA. However, the second balanced his learning by getting involved in campus activities and had some relevant work experience; the 4.0 GPA did nothing but study very hard. To keep it simple, let's assume both were studying business and were marketing majors:

	4.0 GPA	2.0 GPA
Graduating	40	40
Grades	10	6
Time-management skills	8	9
People-management/leadership skills	4	8
Verbal communication skills	5	8
Written communication skills	9	9
Relevant work experience	3	9
TOTAL	79	89

Who would you pick? Can you now see how important it is to balance your formal and informal learning?

And let's remember Bob from chapter 2. What did he do? After he got over the shock of minimum wage, he set a goal to become an electrician, went to college to study electrical engineering, worked for the contractor gaining valuable work experience, and managed to earn a solid living when he graduated.

In the real world today, graduating from a postsecondary program (especially with a degree or diploma related to your desired field) serves as a filter to separate those students who made the investment in time and money to get advanced learning from those who did not. Grades play a minimal role in most hiring decisions (although that varies somewhat by field). Relevant experience also separates those who invested time to develop critical skills and experience from those who did not.

Let me give you another example from my professional experience to really illustrate how these filters work. In companies like Nestlé or Coca-Cola, you can bet there is a lot of competition for any position, whether sales, marketing, finance, production, or operations. One year at Coca-Cola, we were creating a new department and wanted to hire twelve entry-level salespeople. The positions provided a base salary of $35,000, bonus potential for another $5000 per year, plus a company car. Guess how many applications we got from a three-day newspaper advertisement? If you guessed 2,500, you are right.

With so many applications, where do you think we started? We could not interview everyone, as that would take over a year, and we had to have the positions filled in thirty days. Well, first, we looked at each resumé (we really did) and filtered out anyone who had not graduated with a postsecondary degree or diploma. That took 2,000 people off the pile and into the recycling bin. I'll bet you that most of those people could have done a good job, but because they did not graduate with a postsecondary degree or diploma, they never even got a shot.

Now, we still had a pile of five hundred. What did we do next? We then looked through the experience levels of each person. We preferred people with sales and marketing backgrounds. We had many applicants who had a lot of sales experience apply, and we also had many soon-to-be college graduates and recent graduates apply with relevant experience from part-time and summer jobs. We narrowed the list down to fifty people to interview, split about 50/50 between the two groups I just mentioned.

After the interviews, we narrowed it down to a group of fifteen people. Then, guess what we did. We called all of the colleges they said they had graduated from. Did we call to find out their grades? No! We called to verify the applicants actually graduated. Guess what we found out? Three of the people had lied. What happened to them? If you said "bye bye," you are right. We ended up with our twelve people by using college and experience to filter a list of 2,500 people down to the number we needed.

I should also note that in another hiring decision for a manager position a couple of years later, it came down to two equally qualified candidates. What was the tiebreaker? Their grade point average in college. While grades may not play a big role in many hiring decisions, they still play an important role. The better your grades, the less you have to worry about if you have balanced your formal and informal learning.

TIME

A couple of paragraphs ago, I mentioned the concept of "time" as it relates to preparing for life after school, and the role of graduating, grades, and getting experience. Time is really your most precious resource, as employers will be looking to see if you "invested" it wisely to prepare to develop your skills and experience for life after school, or "spent" it on things like partying, playing on the Internet, or sitting around watching TV.

Now, nothing says that you cannot have some fun. If you work hard, it is OK to play hard too. Just do not lose sight of your goals and the need to get a balanced education. Do not become one of the college juniors about to go into their senior year who panic because there is nothing on their resumés related to relevant experience or skills. These people do everything they can to stack their resumé, and guess what? They usually get burned, because they have no accomplishments to back up what they wrote down. Most employers with college recruiters can weed these people out in the first ten minutes of interviewing. Don't be one of them! Take two to four hours per week to devote to volunteer work or working at a part-time job related to your field of interest, and you will be way ahead of most other students today.

It is funny, but over the years I have often heard a lot of students watch others get great jobs and career opportunities and say, "Oh, that person was just lucky!" But what is luck? *Luck is what happens when preparation meets opportunity.* There is an irony here, and that is that the people who make the "Oh, they were just lucky" comments are usually the ones who "spent" their precious school time on unimportant and frivolous things. They are usually just jealous of those who "invested" time. Don't be the whiner . . . be the winner!

CHAPTER SUMMARY

- A degree or diploma serves as a filter between those who completed a postsecondary education from those who did not.
- While good grades are important, grades alone will not determine who gets the best career opportunities.

- Students need to invest time in building relevant skills and experience instead of spending it on unproductive tasks, to build a competitive advantage.
- Relevant experience and skill sets brought to a prospective employer serve as a filter between those who invested time and those who did not.
- Students will go up against a rating scale when they finish their postsecondary education. Fifty points will go to formal learning and fifty points to informal learning. Both are equally important.
- A C-student can beat an A-student if he graduates and has a higher level of developed skills.
- Luck is what happens when preparation meets opportunity.

APPLICATION

- In the example highlighted between the 4.0 and 2.0 GPA students, what would happen if the 4.0 GPA student had also built compatible skills and experience? Who would get the position then?
- If you were to graduate today and applied for a position with ten other students also graduating from your school who have an interest in the same area, how confident are you in your grades and experience that you would get an interview?
- What if you were competing against ten students from across your city about whom you knew nothing? From across your state? From across the country? How confident are you that you would get an interview, let alone the position?
- Think a few years down the road. You are going up against these same students, except they graduated from a postsecondary institution and you did not. How good are your chances in getting an interview now?
- What if you were up against these same students, yet you graduated with a degree or diploma related to the field, had good grades, and also had worked in a related part-time or summer job? How confident would you be in your chances of getting an interview and landing the position?

5

Getting Relevant Experience by Investing Time

In the last chapter, I discussed at length the need to invest time over an extended period to build up relevant experience and skills for your desired field. This extended period of time should be while you are going through high school and college, not after. If you are serious about this and really want to make a good living when you graduate, then there are three ways you can build the skills and experience you need to be successful:

- Work experience
- Cocurricular activities
- Extracurricular activities.

WORK EXPERIENCE

First, let's talk about work experience. This is something of critical importance because:

- It helps you learn about things that you like to do, and if you are going to work for the rest of your life, you will be much more successful doing things you like versus things you dislike.
- It can add tremendous value in helping you to build a competitive advantage in securing the best employment opportunities if it is relevant to your desired field.

• It allows you to develop critical skills such as interpersonal, time, people, leadership, and stress management.

I suspect you are asking yourself right now, "Yeah, great, but how can I find a position in a desired field when I don't know what that is?" After reading the next chapter on getting focused, you should not worry about that question, because the question will then become, "How do I get relevant work experience in my desired field?" There are three ways:

1. Find a job through the newspaper or Internet.
2. Create your own opportunities via networking or starting your own business.
3. Get into a cooperative education program.

First, you can find a lot of jobs in the newspaper and on the internet. Look for jobs related to the field you want to work in and apply. However, one thing you will find is that a lot of part-time, full-time, and student jobs are not advertised. How do you find out about them? Remember the word "networking"!

Many employers often ask good employees for referrals to find new hires. Word of mouth is as important in finding good employees as it is in getting a recommendation from your friends on whether to see a certain movie. When I was in high school, every job I found was from networking and referrals. First, my sister got me into the restaurant where she worked, washing dishes. Then my friend down the street told me about an opening at the local newspaper working in the mailroom. He gave me his boss's name; I called him and got the job. While at the newspaper, my cousin told me about the need for a driver at the Chinese restaurant where she worked, and as I could get paid to drive around and crank tunes, I did this (while also working at the newspaper). Then, my high school buddy told me they needed someone at the local mall where he worked to help do maintenance and security.

Wow! A chance for me to work at the biggest mall in town and chat with all the girls was too good a chance to pass up. I quit the newspaper and Chinese restaurant, because I could get all the hours I wanted at the mall. I started college while working at the mall, and, as I was studying business and wanted relevant experience, I asked the mall's general manager after my freshman year if I could help him with anything. I wanted to apply what I learned in college. He assigned me to organize a big promotion, which I did. I also did painting jobs on the side and made friends with the people working at the student employment center. Guess who got the first call when good painting jobs came in? Do you get the idea of how networking helped me find jobs?

Another way to network is to knock on doors. You read correctly! If people do not come to you, you go to them. A good example is someone I knew from high school. His name was Tony. He was always into cars. He liked fixing dents more than engines and wanted to make it his career, so he went to a community college to learn more. He looked in the paper (the Internet had not yet been launched at that time) for a part-time job at a body shop, but the only jobs he could find were full-time, and in another city thirty miles away. He could have quit school, but like Bob, the electrician we discussed earlier, he would be making minimum wage, because he had not graduated from college with his auto body diploma.

Frustrated, and knowing he wanted to work on cars, Tony took matters into his own hands. He looked in the yellow pages and found five auto body shops in town. He hopped in his car on a day off from school and drove to each one, asking the owner if they were hiring. Each time he was told "No." To Tony, "No" meant "Not yet."

One week later, he drove back to each shop to speak with the owners again and said, "I know you don't have a job open, but I am studying auto body at the community college and want to see what you do to apply what I am learning in school. Could I come in on Saturday mornings, stand off to the side, and watch what you do? I won't get in the way."

The first four shops he went to said "No" again, but when he went to the last one, guess what happened? The owner said "Yes!" For the next month, every Saturday morning, Tony went to the shop, stood off to the side, and watched. And then guess what happened? One of the guys called in sick, and the owner called Tony over to help put a bumper back on a car. When they were doing this, Tony knew exactly what to do. There was a backlog of cars needing to be fixed, and the owner said to Tony "OK, kid, how would you like to work part-time on Saturdays?" Tony was excited! He got $10/hour, badly needed money for school, plus relevant work experience. When summer came after his first year, guess who worked full-time at the shop?

What is the moral of the story? Get used to rejection, but if you really want something, perseverance will always prevail. Remember when we discussed those people who call others lucky? What did we say luck was? Luck is what happens when preparation meets opportunity, and Tony created his own opportunity!

Now, another way that you can get paid to get relevant work experience plus study in your desired field is through cooperative (co-op) education programs. Co-op programs usually allow you to study one semester, then work one semester with an employer in your desired field. Co-op programs are becoming increasingly popular today. When you plan to check colleges out, see if they offer a co-op program. If you can get into the program, you will be ahead of the pack, because these programs enable you to get exposure to companies, and vice versa, and many people end up getting hired full-time by the companies they interned with.

If you can't get paid to get experience, don't worry. There are two more options available that can pay off in a big way come graduation day.

COCURRICULAR AND EXTRACURRICULAR ACTIVITIES

Cocurricular and extracurricular activities are two great ways to invest a few hours per week to build up relevant experience and critical skills. It requires volunteering your time to get involved. What's the difference between the two?

"Cocurricular" means activities you can get involved with at school before, during, or after school hours. Good examples are athletics, student government, clubs, or the band. "Extracurricular" means activities you can get involved with off campus, like helping a local charity, volunteering at a seniors' center, or maybe helping the campaign of a local politician. Try to pick things that will help you down the road or open some networking opportunities in your desired career area.

For example, getting involved in cocurricular activities, especially student council and clubs, is something a lot of employers take notice of, especially if you held an executive position like president or vice president. Remember the critical skills of networking, leadership, time management, and communication? You can learn all of these by getting involved. Now, many kids get positions for the sake of a cool title for their resumé but can't back it up with any accomplishments. If you actually do something in the position, potential employers will be more impressed. It will demonstrate you took initiative, applied yourself, and learned how to work with others to get things done (as opposed to being a club member, just showing up for meetings).

One of the main reasons I got into Coca-Cola was because I had been elected vice president of seminars for the Marketing Club. We wanted someone from Coca-Cola to come in and speak to our members. I organized the event, yet had no idea who was coming to speak. The night of the seminar we held elections for the next school year. I was running for president. I did not know it at the time, but as I was up doing my speech, our guest speaker arrived. He was the chief operating officer (COO)—the #2 person in the company. He heard the whole thing.

As his secretary had had kind things to say about me in organizing the event, and as he heard my speech, when I asked him how I could get into Coca-Cola for a summer position before my senior year, and possibly full-time afterwards, his answer was, "Send me your resumé and I'll see what I can do" (buzzword: networking). I sent him my resumé, and he called the local operation to see if there were any jobs I could fill. If you were the general manager who received a call from your boss's boss's boss, do you think you would say you could not find anything? While I could not get a sales position, they did offer me a job slugging cases on a truck. I called the COO to thank him. He asked me to keep in touch during my senior year. I not only kept in touch with him, I kept in touch with his assistant too (whom I still keep in touch with to this day . . . we became good friends). When it came time to graduate, the local operation created a job for me at the same time he was creating a position at headquarters. I fulfilled my dream of getting into a company, which at that time was the most respected and desired employer for graduating students in sales and marketing. Many of my classmates called me lucky, but you know what luck is: it is what happens when preparation meets opportunity. Seize every opportunity you can!

RUNNING FOR AN ELECTION

We have discussed possibly running for an elected position with a volunteer organization. To get to a leadership position in a club or student council, like the Marketing Club I was in, running in an election will likely become a reality. That means doing speeches, placing posters, and networking. Don't sweat it! Give it your best shot, and guess what? Whether you win or lose, you just enhanced your public speaking and organizational skills, something many employers like.

Now, times have not changed that much over the years. When I was in high school, a lot of "cool" kids thought that running for an election made you look like a dork, dweeb, or a nerd. That is OK. They are entitled to an opinion. But let me tell you something from my own personal experience: Those "cool" kids in high school never really amounted to much afterward. Last I heard, the good-looking former captain of our high school football team was fat, bald, and on welfare. And the former head cheerleader was divorced, trying to raise three children on tips from waiting tables. So, if it means you take a little heat from people who end up becoming total losers, hey, after you graduate, you will be earning a solid living and you can wave to them in your new car while they are still taking the bus!

Don't let anyone talk you out of getting involved in cocurricular or extracurricular activities if you want to, because there are a lot of benefits. You can learn and develop valuable time, stress, people, interpersonal, leadership, and management skills for *free* (with the exception of your time), plus learn how to network. You can apply what you learn in books, and although you may not get paid while you are volunteering, the payoff will be there come graduation day, because you built a competitive advantage and made yourself more desirable to potential employers. Do not take on so much that it will affect your studies, and don't try to do everything in a short period of time. Life is not a hundred-yard race, it is a marathon. Pace yourself, balance your learning, have some fun, and you will be well on your way to a happy and prosperous life.

Now, the one question that still needs to be answered is: To which employers do I want to make myself desirable? To answer that, you have to answer reality check question #2: Where do I want to go? We have already laid out the things you need to do to get there. To do that, you have to answer one more very important question, probably the most important question ever: What would I love to do for the rest of my life?

Trust me on this one: If you do something you love, success to some extent, no matter how you define it, will always follow. In the next chapter, we will review many ways to help you get focused to answer this question so you can build a competitive advantage to have your choice of great opportunities upon graduating.

CHAPTER SUMMARY

- Work experience, cocurricular activities, and extracurricular activities can help you build all of the relevant skills and experience you need.
- Cocurricular activities are activities you can get involved with at school.
- Extracurricular activities are activities you can get involved with off campus in your community.
- Invest some time to build relevant skills and experience. Volunteering does not pay at the time you do it, but the payoff could be huge come graduation.
- Don't be afraid to run for an elected position. The experience you gain will be well worth it, as holding a leadership position is always preferred by employers.
- Many positions are not advertised. Networking skills are critical to finding some of the best opportunities.
- Cooperative education programs let you study then work a semester. They are a great way to get relevant studies and experience, not to mention cash.
- Don't be afraid of getting involved, as employers want to hire people with relevant experience.

APPLICATION

- Why is relevant work experience so important?
- What is the difference between cocurricular and extracurricular activities?
- In chapter 2, I asked you to think about a future career goal. How could getting involved in cocurricular or extracurricular activities help you get there?

- What steps can you take today to help you build your experience and critical skills?
- What did Tony do that was so different from so many students today? How was he able to get relevant experience in his desired field?
- In chapter 3 we discussed formal and informal learning and illustrated how your learning retention would be much higher if you could apply what you have learned. Have you ever learned something in a book that you applied at work or through an activity? If so, what was it? Why do you still remember it today?

6

Getting Focused on Your Future

Career success really starts to take shape when individuals are not only well prepared for a particular field or occupational area but passionate about it. One of the biggest reasons young people today are frustrated in finding great employment opportunities is that they enter the workforce with little idea about what they want to do with the rest of their life. This chapter will focus on how you can be one of those people who is focused. (Note: You may want to read this chapter twice.)

I want to again bring back the three reality check questions we discussed in chapter 1. Do you remember what they were?

1. Where am I now?
2. Where do I want to go?
3. How am I going to get there?

I also asked, "Where do you see yourself in twenty-five years?" and gave you a pyramid to help you determine that. Since then, we have discussed the difference between a job and career; the importance of balancing your formal and informal learning; the role of degrees, grades, and relevant experience; critical skills employers are looking for; and the rating scale employers use come graduation day. We just discussed the importance of work experience, cocurricular activities, and extracurricular activities. It is now time to pull it all together to discuss how you can get focused on your future in order to build a competitive advantage and secure not only an opportunity in your desired field but have your choice of opportunities.

SOME VERY IMPORTANT FORMULAS

A few years ago, I read the following formulas (from Roberto Goizuetta in *Journey* magazine, March 1994) and have never forgotten them:

Motivation − Direction = Frustration
Mission + Commitment = Focus
Focus + Action = Results.

When I asked you at the opening of this book if you wanted to make at least $40,000/year, I'll bet you said "Yes." If I asked you right now, "In what type of career will you be successful?" I will bet most of you either still do not know, or can only guess (a couple of exercises in earlier chapters should have helped to get you thinking about your future).

I have not met many students who do not want to make lots of money when they graduate. I have met more than I can count who were upset because they graduated and were frustrated in finding an employment opportunity in their desired field, or worse, finding any decent full-time opportunity at all. Why? Unlike a ship that plots a course to go in a certain direction, these individuals did not take the time to answer reality check questions #2 and #3 and get focused while in school.

Being motivated yet not pursuing a specific direction will always lead to frustration. So how do you minimize frustration? Get focused! To be focused, you must have a mission and be committed to achieving it. Another word for "mission" is "goal." Set some goals that are relevant to you and what you want to do, and becoming committed to achieving your goals is almost guaranteed.

Once you are focused, the only thing missing is the effort to balance your formal and informal learning to achieve your goals. Focus plus action will always get results. As someone once told me, "A vision without an action is just a dream." The better the focus, the more time invested to study a field you love and in which you gain relevant skills and experience, the better your level of success will be.

INFLUENCES ON YOUR FUTURE: FAMILY AND FRIENDS

Getting focused requires that you learn a lot about yourself. That means learning what you like, what you dislike, and understanding what your strengths and weaknesses are, as well as what developmental opportunities lie ahead of you and what threats could block you from achieving your goals. Your past experiences help to shape who you are and who you want to be. And as it relates to going to college, your future goals and aspirations may be just a dream because of your current academic or economic situation. We will discuss both in the next chapter, but first I want to discuss in greater detail two very important influences in your life right now that will play an important role in your future.

Your friends and your family play big roles in your life today. As individuals, it is human nature to listen to what they have to say. Whenever I do speeches for your teachers, counselors, and principals, I always ask them two questions:

1. Have you ever seen a student who passed up the chance to go to college, or to a better college, because they wanted to continue to date a certain boyfriend or girlfriend, or to continue to hang out with their friends?
2. Have you ever seen a student who was passionate about pursuing a certain career, only to have their parents override their dreams by stating, "No way are you going to be this, you are going to be that" or "You are not going to that college because everyone in our family has always gone to this college!"?

Guess how many teachers, counselors, and principals raised their hands? Every single one of them!

High school is a great time—some will argue, the best time of your life. You will meet many people, some of whom you will develop lifelong friendships with. However, as the years go on, people go their own ways. People go to college, get married, start careers, move all over the country, sometimes overseas. Remember one thing: They will not be interviewing for jobs on your behalf! Only you can, and your ability to be the #1 candidate will be based on how well *you* prepared.

As it relates to families, we don't pick them, we are born into them. Some students have supporting, loving parents, while others live with control freaks who yell and scream a lot. Until you turn eighteen, your parents are responsible for you. Growing up with them every day means they exert a tremendous amount of influence on your life. We often will ask them their advice on issues, and sometimes they give advice whether we want it or not. But remember one thing: it is advice. At the end of the day, only you can make the choice to accept or reject it. You will also have to apply yourself and accept full responsibility for the decisions you make and the outcomes.

I'll give you two quick examples of advice my father gave me to illustrate how I had to make some tough choices. In one case I listened, in the other I did not. First, when I turned thirteen, my father sat me down at the kitchen table and gave me a quiz to see if I knew the difference between right and wrong. He asked me questions like "Breaking into someone's house: right or wrong?" and "Doing drugs: right or wrong?" I answered "Wrong," and I was right. He then said something to me I will never forget. He said, "As you go to high school, your friends will push you sometimes to do things that are wrong. I won't be there to watch over you, you will have to make decisions for yourself. If the police catch you doing something wrong, don't bother calling me. As life is about choices, you made the decision to do the wrong thing instead of walking away and doing the right thing. If you can get yourself into the mess, you are smart enough to figure out how to get yourself out of it." On many occasions over my teenage years, I found myself in situations having to decide to do the right or wrong thing. His words always echoed in my ears, and I tried to make the right choices every time.

However, when I was preparing to go to college and figure out what I wanted to do for the rest of my life, the situation was very different. In elementary school, I always told my father I wanted to be a lawyer, but by high school it did not interest me any more. I wanted to be in the business world. When I told my father I wanted to study political science and history (but I failed to tell him I didn't want to go to law school), he stated, "If you want to get into the business world, do you think it would be better to have a business degree or a history degree? At least study business. If you don't get into law school, it will be much stronger to fall back on." You know what? He was right!

I always liked sales and marketing and decided to pursue a career in that field. When I was a sophomore in college, I finally broke the news to my father that I did not want to go to law school. That night, I listened to a long lecture about how "sales" was not a real profession and that if I wasn't going to be a lawyer, I "should be an accountant . . . that's where the big bucks are." I politely excused myself from the table, telling my father, "You always taught me to make smart choices and trust my instincts. As I am going to have to work for the rest of my life, I really want to do something that I love! If you love accounting so much, you become the accountant! As for me, this is the direction I want to go in." It was tough walking away because my dad had given me great advice to study business, but I had to draw the line on the accounting advice and stick to what I was passionate about.

When high school is over, please do not put your future on hold because of your friends or family. You can listen to their opinions, but at the end of the day, the choices are ultimately yours. You only have yourself to blame if you do not make smart choices. By smart choices, I mean pursuing what you are passionate about rather than what someone else wants you to do (including staying out of trouble). You cannot blame anyone but yourself if you see others getting opportunities you want, either. While it may be tough, sometimes you may have to stand up to your friends and family if you think you are right about your future choices.

When you are in your thirties and see your high school friends maybe once every couple of years or at your reunions, and your parents are getting ready for retirement, traveling, and having fun, are either of them going to care that you gave up the chance to pursue a career path when you were a teenager that you were passionate about in favor of what they wanted you to do? Absolutely not! Make smart choices today, get focused, and apply yourself so that you will be grateful ten, twenty, thirty, even forty years from now! If you do not, be prepared to suck it up when your friends and family ask why you have not accomplished anything and then tell you, "I told you so . . . you should have listened to me."

THREE EXERCISES TO GET YOU FOCUSED

As we talked about earlier in this chapter, getting focused, setting goals, and putting actions behind them will get you results. Getting focused is the critical element in answering reality check question #2: Where do I want to go?

Getting to where you want to go is easy once you know what you want to do. To help you figure that out, I want to walk you through three short exercises that you should do before you ever walk into your counselor's office to discuss career options. First, please look at the chart on the next page. I call it the Like/Dislike Model.

Take about a half-hour one day and just think—think about what you like and dislike as it relates to subjects in school (formal learning), and what you like and dislike in people, part-time jobs, friends, music, and so on (informal learning).

Step 2 is writing them down in a simple T-chart like the one in figure 6.2 on page 44. During a very boring (in my opinion only) math class, I did this exercise in my senior year in high school. It was the best hour I ever spent in school, because I learned a lot about myself.

As it relates to your formal learning, focus on the courses you really like, because if you go to college, you will usually do as well or better in courses that you like. You will usually do as well or worse in courses that you dislike.

As it relates to informal learning, one piece of advice I would like to share with you is this: During high school and early in college, try to get exposure to many different industries. I worked in restaurants, at the local newspaper, at the mall, and at a manufacturing company. I had washed dishes, cooked, run a press, driven a truck, and done maintenance and security, as well as sales and marketing research.

Working in a variety of areas and industries helped me to figure out that if I was going to work the rest of my life, I would rather use my brains than my muscles. I learned that I was most passionate about sales and marketing, and I focused on that for my career. I also learned a lot about what type of people I wanted to be around.

After you have examined your likes and dislikes, take it one step farther by doing a "SWOT analysis." When I was in college studying business, we did case studies of companies that did well and not so well and used SWOT every time. It is a process where you examine strengths, weaknesses, opportunities, and threats. After doing a case study, I thought it would be an interesting exercise to do a SWOT on myself. Thank

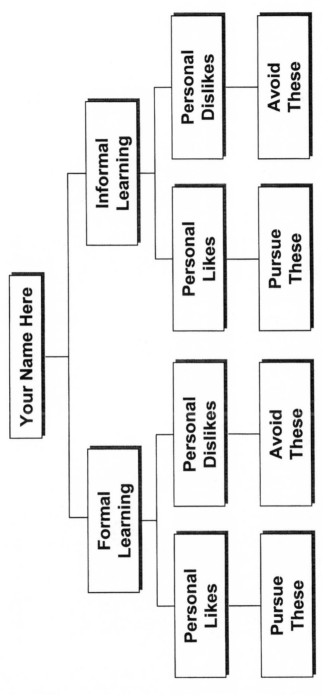

Figure 6.1.   The Like/Dislike Model

LIKES

- being creative

- marketing, history, English

- dealing with honest, polite people

- driving a car

- working with people

- business

- hockey, tennis, cycling, golf

- cranking tunes on my stereo

- AC/DC, Ramones, Neil Young

- sales and marketing jobs

DISLIKES

- people who discourage creativity

- calculus and physics courses

- dealing with selfish egomaniacs

- public transportation

- working construction

- bosses who are jerks

- jogging, gymnastics

- Dad cranking his tunes

- opera music

- washing dishes

Figure 6.2.   Likes and Dislikes T-Chart Exercise

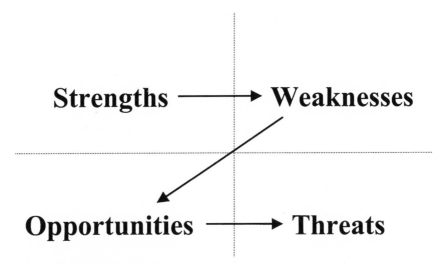

Figure 6.3. SWOT Analysis

heaven I did, because it helped me to learn even more about the things I still needed to do to build a competitive advantage for graduation day.

Doing a SWOT analysis is a little harder than the Like/Dislike exercise, because strengths help you identify weaknesses. Figure 6.3 above illustrates this. Understanding both will help you get focused on your opportunities for development. If you understand your opportunities for development, you will be able to identify potential threats and barriers that may block you from achieving your goals.

As discussed above, my Like/Dislike exercises helped me to get focused on a career in sales and marketing. As a result, I went to college to study business (formal learning). My SWOT analysis, as shown in figure 6.4 on the next page, helped me focus on things that would help me build my experience and skill sets to be successful in sales and marketing after graduation (informal learning).

When I did my SWOT, you will notice that the items were related. For example, a strength of mine was that I liked working with people. As I aspired to "move up the ladder," I realized one of my weaknesses was that I lacked leadership skills. My opportunity for development was to build leadership skills. My threat was that there were many other students on my campus whom I might have to compete with to secure leadership positions.

SWOT ANALYSIS

Strengths	*Weaknesses*
- dealing with people - history, English, marketing - good mind for business - like to be challenged - independent thinker	- lack leadership skills - hate math, science - afraid of a dead-end job - lack time/stress-management skills - sometimes I don't listen to others
Opportunities	*Threats*
- get involved in cocurricular activities - enter a business program - get a college degree - learn time/stress-management skills - improve my listening skills	- competition for leadership positions - failing math, computers, finance - losing chance at great jobs if I failed - burning out and losing interest - Dad still wants me to be an accountant

Figure 6.4. Personal SWOT Analysis

See how it flows? Please go through each point on my SWOT, as all of the points line up with each other—point 1 in all SWOT categories aligns, point 2 aligns, etc. This will give you an idea of how to complete this exercise.

Doing the Like/Dislike and SWOT exercises will help you get focused. They will help you answer reality check questions #2 and #3 (Where do I want to go? How am I going to get there?). They will help you lay out a road map so that you will be motivated, not frustrated, and be focused on things you like and are passionate about. Completing this process is a pre-requisite for success upon entering the workforce.

What's the final link in the chain? It is up to you to put actions behind your goals to get your desired results related to balancing your formal and informal learning. It is that simple! It will be a combination of your post-secondary studies and investment in skill-set building that will set you apart from the rest. As was once said to me, "The difference between the 'best' and the 'rest' is that the best keep getting better." It is not a question of whether there are great opportunities out there; the question always comes down to who will claim them. Give it your best!

A PERSONAL NOTE

I was not certain whether to include the following in this book, but given our recent discussion about friends and family, I want to share two personal comments that I hope you will take into serious consideration over the next few years. First, please do not do something so stupid that it will result in a criminal record. Nothing kills career opportunities faster than that. Second, please do not do something so stupid as drinking and driving. When I was in high school, there was a lot of peer pressure to try drugs or alcohol. It is sad, but I was flipping through all of my high school yearbooks recently, and every single edition had an "In Memoriam" page to students from my high school who were killed in car accidents on weekend nights. One of the accidents was caused by our student council president, who subsequently spent two years in jail. At least he eventually got to go home, unlike the person in the other car, who didn't survive. Never put yourself in any situation where your future, and others' lives, will be at risk. Not only will it hurt your future, it will hurt the futures of the families impacted too.

CHAPTER SUMMARY

- Learning about yourself can help you get you focused. Being focused means you are less likely to be frustrated. Using actions to support your focus means you will get better results than those who just think about things.
- Identifying your likes and dislikes can help you discover what you are passionate about.
- Doing something you are passionate about, rather than something you hate, will always lead to greater career satisfaction.
- Using SWOT analysis to identify your strengths, weaknesses, opportunities, and threats helps you to build action plans in support of your likes and dislikes.
- Going through these important exercises can help you answer the three reality check questions.
- Friends and family have a tremendous influence over your future. It is OK to listen to their point of view, but remember, when you are

forty years old, you can only blame yourself if you pursued a path just to keep them happy when you were eighteen.

APPLICATION

- Draw the Like/Dislike T-bar and look at the Like/Dislike model. Take a few minutes to write down things you like regarding your formal learning and informal learning.
- Can you think of one to three possible career areas that relate to your likes?
- Do a SWOT analysis related to your possible career area. What are your strengths? Weaknesses? Opportunities? Threats?
- What are the three reality check questions?
- Can you answer question 2 now? Where do I want to go?
- Examining what employers are looking for (chapter 2), the importance of balancing formal and informal learning, and building relevant experience and skills, lay out five to ten steps that you can take to help you get to where you want to go.
- If you completed the last exercise, congratulations, because you just laid out an action plan to answer reality check question #3: How am I going to get there? What will you do if your friends, boyfriend/girlfriend, or family object to your choice?

7

Going to College and Education Costs

In the last chapter, we discussed getting focused, setting goals, and applying yourself to achieving those goals by identifying your likes, dislikes, strengths, weaknesses, opportunities, and threats. In earlier chapters, we discussed the importance of balancing your formal and informal learning. While I have focused on building your informal learning in prior chapters, in this chapter, I want to really focus on the formal learning part. After all, it is 50 percent of the rating scale employers will be putting you up against.

Knowing what you like and are passionate about is very important. So too is knowing your SWOT. But if you cannot get into a postsecondary institution to advance your studies in your desired career area, these will be just "good to know" items. So let's take a look at some important topics related to getting into college and covering the costs of your postsecondary education.

WHAT COLLEGES ARE LOOKING FOR

College attendance has increased dramatically over the past two decades. People preparing to join the workforce now realize, more than ever, that employers have a lot of people to choose from and that they want to hire the best, regardless of the field. Whether it is repairing cars, nursing, accounting, physical therapy, or running a restaurant, there is a postsecondary institution (university, community college, career college, technical school) that can help you get advanced level of studies in your desired field.

In today's environment, most colleges will look at four primary things when deciding on whom to admit. They are:

1. Grade point average
2. SAT/ACT scores
3. Reference letters
4. Writing samples.

First, let's talk about your grade point average. In the old days, colleges used to admit whoever could pay for it. Grade point averages in the C range were not uncommon. Today, the story is very different. Based on several schools I surveyed, if you want a strong shot at getting into the college and program of your choice, make certain your grades are in the B range or better. To validate this, UCLA does a survey of incoming freshman students. For the past several years, over 99 percent of students admitted to UCLA have had averages of B or better. At other public postsecondary institutions, that number was over 85 percent. If your grades are below that, it is time to pull up your socks!

Second, your SATs or ACTs will be important. The higher the score, the better. Colleges will look at students above certain levels as their first choices (e.g., over 1000), but these standardized tests will often not be the deciding factor. What will be? Reference letters and your writing skills!

Students often do not take reference letters seriously. But talk to admission officers, and many will tell you that they accepted or rejected certain candidates because of the strength of the reference letters. They have often used them as tiebreakers as well when it comes down to final admission decisions.

Also, according to several educators I spoke with, postsecondary institutions are looking more closely at the writing skills of applicants via samples submitted. If the skills are strong but the SATs or ACTs are not as strong, consideration for admission may still be given.

Your grades, SAT/ACT scores, reference letters, and writing samples will help you get into college, but once there, you need to stay. That will be contingent on two things: your academics and your ability to cover your education costs. Let's look at both of these areas a little more closely.

EDUCATION COSTS

First, let's start with education costs. I want you to think for a moment about what all of the costs associated with your postsecondary education are. Take thirty seconds right now to write down the costs you think you may encounter before we proceed any further.

Are you finished with the exercise? Good. Now, at this time, I would like to share a very simple formula that highlights the associated costs of a postsecondary education. It looks something like this:

Actual Financial Costs

+

Education Opportunity Costs

=

Education Costs

I'll bet you didn't think that a formula was necessary, because most students only think education costs are related to actual financial costs, like tuition, rent, meals, books, transportation, and entertainment expenses. However, there are other costs that need to be examined more closely, and these are the education opportunity costs.

What Are Education Opportunity Costs?

They are extra costs incurred by those who have to complete, for some reason, extra semesters or years of study to graduate from a postsecondary education. Almost every adult I know can think of at least one person who was on the "seven-year plan" (who needed seven years to graduate from college). There are three types of people who bear education opportunity costs, usually for two primary reasons. It can be easily illustrated in the chart on the next page.

Moving away from parents is a great experience. Staying out as late as you want, dating whomever you want, and keeping your room as messy as you want are just some of the pluses. But don't forget why you went to college. You are going so that you can balance your formal and informal learning and build a competitive advantage to secure your desired career opportunities upon graduation.

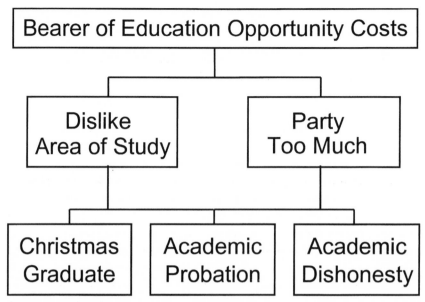

Figure 7.1.   Education Opportunity Costs

Most people who have encountered opportunity costs either partied too much or they were in a program they hated. To be honest, the majority of people partied too much because that first taste of freedom was just too tempting.

Going out with friends, instead of keeping up with homework, became the priority. That is why, in college, instructors weight assignments so low, and the exams so high, as it relates to the final grade. The grade point average really separates those who did their homework and knew their stuff from those who copied the assignments of others and did not study. This leads us to looking at the three types of people who bear education opportunity costs.

Who Bears Education Opportunity Costs?

There are typically three categories of students who bear education opportunity costs:

1. *The Christmas graduate.* These are the freshman students who never went to a single class and hung out at the campus pub every day.

They had no grade point average, because they failed every class. As a result, they packed up and moved home for the holidays in December. (Trying to find on-campus housing is next to impossible in August or September. It is very easy in January.) My own personal observation: Many of these students had no stake in paying for their college—it was Mom's or Dad's money. Those who were contributing to their own education rarely dropped out.

2. Those on *academic probation*. These are students of all levels (freshmen, sophomores, juniors) who show up to a few classes and have a grade point average but are given by their school or faculty either one semester or a school year to pull up their grades. If not, they are expelled.

3. Those convicted of *academic dishonesty*. You do not want to be a student caught cheating in college. Think twice before you go the lazy way of copying someone else's essay or text-messaging an answer to a friend during an exam. Teachers and professors do keep copies of old essays and assignments. During exams, monitors closely watch everyone. Get caught cheating and you are expelled! A notation is also put on your academic record, and you must wait five years to get it removed through an appeals process, much like a convict asking for parole. You may try to lie to other schools and apply, but they will run a computer check. If caught stretching the truth again, you are now expelled a second time from another school, and your grave just got that much deeper.

AN EDUCATION OPPORTUNITY COST STORY

To illustrate the "opportunity costs" of avoidable extra semesters of studies, let me give you a real-life example of two students who both entered a four-year college business program. We'll call them Frick and Frack.

Frick and Frack were both freshmen at the same college and had graduated with the same grades from the same high school from the same hometown. Both wanted to get into the School of Business, which required one year of undergraduate work with no failed courses and a minimum grade point average of a B prior to admission. Once admitted, there were three years of studies required to graduate with the business degree.

Frick decided to live on campus in a dorm, as his mom and dad had saved some money for his college education. Frack, on the other hand, commuted from home because she was paying for college all by herself, as her parents struggled just to pay the bills. The money she saved on rent went to pay for tuition and other expenses.

Frick and Frack both studied, yet Frick spent a lot more time at the campus pub than Frack. Frick started to leave homework to the last minute because going out with his friends was more important. Frack went out with her friends too, but not until her homework was done. At the end of their freshman year, Frack was accepted into the School of Business, but Frick was expelled because he had failed two courses.

Frick took some general courses during their sophomore year, while Frack was in the School of Business. As Frack was entering her junior year, Frick reapplied to the Business faculty. In order to be readmitted, he had to re-complete every freshman course to qualify for the School of Business. Frack was in her senior year when Frick finally got into the School of Business.

At the end of the year, Frack graduated, balanced her formal and informal learning, and landed a great career opportunity with a well-known company, making $40,000 per year. Frick was now three years behind Frack and was out of money. He went to school part-time, worked part-time, and made $10,000 to get enough cash to finish college because he already had racked up $25,000 in student loans. Enjoying his summer vacations had been more important than getting a summer job, unlike for Frack, who worked part-time during the school year and always worked in the summer. Frick's parents had also ran out of money to support his education. Frick finally graduated, but that was three years after Frack did . . . on the seven-year plan.

When Frick joined the workforce, Frack had already earned her first promotion and received a raise to $46,000/year. Let's look at how much those few extra nights of partying cost Frick:

Tuition: 2 years @ $4,000/year = $8,000
Books: 2 years @ $900/year = $1,800
Income lost @ $30,000/year = $90,000 ($40,000−$10,000 = $30,000
    × 3 years behind)
Three extra years' interest on $25,000 student loans = $8,000.

Conservatively, Frick bore education opportunity costs of over $100,000 compared to Frack. These were the extra expenses paid for avoidable semesters, books, and the real kicker—$90,000 in earning potential lost! Let's not forget that he was also three years behind his good friend in getting a shot at any type of promotional opportunity. And imagine the poor fool who was convicted of academic dishonesty, expelled, and prevented from applying to another college for five years. How much did taking short cuts now cost him or her? Probably double or triple what it cost Frick!

MINIMIZING EDUCATION OPPORTUNITY COSTS

How do you minimize the chances of being in the same situation as Frick and be more like Frack, who found a great career opportunity in her desired field? It comes down to one word: responsibility.

Being responsible means you make the final decisions regarding your future, as you can blame nobody but yourself if others get better opportunities than you. It means you take full ownership to get focused, set goals, and apply yourself to balance your formal and informal learning in order to build a competitive advantage to secure your desired opportunities. If others do better than you, it only means that they wanted success and bigger paychecks more than you. Responsibility means investing time in preparing for life after school, as well as taking full ownership of securing the funds to pay for your college education.

SOURCES OF FUNDS TO PAY ACTUAL FINANCIAL COSTS

Now that you understand the importance of education opportunity costs and minimizing them by being responsible, let's look at sources for finding those badly needed dollars to pay for the actual financial costs: tuition, books, groceries, and rent. There are six possible sources that I would like to share with you:

- Summer and part-time jobs
- Scholarships
- Student loans

- Cooperative education programs
- Military
- Family.

Summer and Part-Time Jobs

Every year, I meet students who cannot find good summer jobs. When I ask them why, in almost every case, it is June and they just started looking. Guess who got the good summer jobs? Those who started looking at Christmas, or spring break at the latest. And guess what? Many of the best jobs are not advertised. I know plenty of students who could not find jobs, so they started calling employers they wanted to work for (recall Tony, the auto body student earlier in the book), or they started their own companies (building websites, painting, etc.).

I recently read a statistic that said over 70 percent of today's students have part-time jobs while they study. A few hours a week of employment can go a long way to help cover some of your bills. Personally, I usually had a part-time job during college and at least two summer jobs. I also never went away for vacations at Christmas, spring break, or in the summer, because for every day I did not work, I lost $50–$75 that I needed to pay for my expenses. As life is about choices, for me it was a choice between spending money and earning it. I opted for covering my bills.

Dilemma: What do you do if you have a summer job opportunity in your desired field but you can get a better paying one doing something else that is not related? My recommendation: As hard as it is, take the one in your desired field. Remember how important relevant experience is in building a competitive advantage and the story of the student who was interviewed by the reporter who was upset about not getting the interview for the $40,000/year marketing job. A student loan can always cover any shortfall, which might be a couple of thousand dollars. In the grand scheme of things, this is a small investment for your future.

Scholarships

Did you know there are over $1 billion in scholarships available today, and grades are not the only prerequisite? Check the Internet for scholarship sites (e.g., www.scholarships101.com).

Student Loans

Given that graduating with a postsecondary education is a requirement for many of the best career opportunities, if you find yourself strapped for cash, get a student loan like millions of other students before you. It is up to you how much you borrow. The more money you make in your summer and part-time jobs, the less you will have to borrow, and the quicker you will be able to pay off your debt!

Cooperative Education Programs

We discussed these earlier in the book. Many colleges have partnered with businesses to create programs whereby you study one semester, then work one semester with an employer related to that career area. What a great way for you to balance your formal and informal learning, not to mention the value of earning cash to pay for your bills.

Military

Do not discount the military as a way to pursue higher education. There are countless stories of individuals who earned enough money for college by serving in the military. And for those interested in the world of big business, you may want to know that in a *Fortune* article of not too long ago looking at the backgrounds of the Top 100 CEOs, the #1 institution for learning was the military (over 30 percent of the Top 100 CEOs had served in the military, where they learned leadership, time, and stress-management skills).

Family

You may notice that I put family last. I did that for a reason. In many households, both parents have to work to pay the bills; however, many of today's youth live in single-parent families. In the old days, a lot of students expected their parents to pay for college. Today, that is a bonus, not the rule. If your parents cannot cover the costs, do not worry—there are five other options noted above that have well served millions of other students before you!

I want to discuss one more option that does not include raising money but rather stretching a college budget. What is the option? Many students with good grades are going to community colleges for a couple of years and then transferring to a university to complete their studies. Why? Community colleges are often local and close to home, enabling students to save money on rent and groceries. The cost per credit is also often much less than at a university. Spending a couple of years at a community college and then going to a university helps to stretch out a tight budget and helps many still get to where they want to go in their desired time frame. Don't discount this option.

Going to some type of postsecondary institution is important. Graduating from that institution is even more important if you want to secure the best employment opportunities. Make certain you make the most of your financial investment. Accept responsibility for your own future, apply yourself to balance your formal and informal learning, do not risk education opportunity costs—and before you know it, doors will be opening for you that others could only hope for. Maximize your choices and opportunities! You can make it happen!

CHAPTER SUMMARY

- Postsecondary institutions are looking for students with good grades, good SATs/ACTs, and strong reference letters.
- Reference letters can be an admissions tiebreaker.
- Writing skills that are strong may help negate not as strong SAT/ACT scores.
- Education costs comprise actual financial costs and education opportunity costs.
- Education opportunity costs are borne by those who have to complete avoidable extra semesters or years of study.
- There are three types of students who bear education opportunity costs: the Christmas graduate, those on academic probation, and those convicted of academic dishonesty. Do not become one of them.
- People who are responsible are less likely to bear education opportunity costs.
- There are six ways to secure funds to pay for a postsecondary education: summer/part-time jobs, scholarships, student loans, cooperative education programs, military service, and your family.

APPLICATION

- Why was Frack more successful than Frick? How much education opportunity cost did Frick bear because he did not have his priorities straight? How would you feel if you were Frack? How would you feel if you were Frick, knowing how much money you threw out the window?
- What is a Christmas graduate?
- What happens to someone put on academic probation?
- What happens to someone convicted of academic dishonesty?
- List three summer jobs you would love to have and three employers you would love to work for. Are there jobs advertised with these employers currently? Are the jobs related to your desired field? What steps can you take today to try to secure one of these jobs with one of your desired employers? (Hint: Tony.)
- If given the choice between a higher-paying summer job in an area not related to your career of choice versus a lower-paying summer job in a related area, which one would you take? Why?
- Have you had part-time or summer jobs? If so, what were they? Would they help you or hurt you in your desired career area? Moving forward, what could you do to build a competitive advantage?
- What ways can you get enough money to pay for college if you have not saved enough from your summer/part-time jobs and your family cannot contribute?

8

Conclusion

When we started this book, I asked you to answer three reality check questions:

1. Where am I now?
2. Where do I want to go?
3. How am I going to get there?

We have covered a lot of topics and exercises that I hope have gotten you to think about life after school and how to build a competitive advantage to secure the best opportunities when you graduate.

Before we wind things up, I want you to ask yourself the following questions to refresh your memory on many things we discussed and to keep you thinking about preparing for life after school. Many can be answered with a "Yes" or "No." It may not be a bad idea to get a piece of paper and write your answers down . . . ready? . . . OK . . . let's go. Ask yourself:

1. Do I want to land a great career opportunity upon graduating making at least $40,000 per year to start?
2. Do I want a job or career? Why?
3. Have I identified my likes/dislikes and refined them using SWOT?
4. Have I developed an interest in a desired field or area (or a few)?
5. What is more important to my future: formal learning or informal learning?

6. Am I prepared to apply myself to balance my formal and informal learning to build a competitive advantage?
7. Do I want to go to a technical school, community college, career college, or university for my formal learning? To study what?
8. Do I currently have the grades to get into the postsecondary program I want?
9. Do I have the money available to attend? If not, how can I get it?
10. What organization can I work for, and/or get involved with, to gain relevant skills and experience for my desired career prior to graduating?

In a nutshell, answering these questions is really asking you to do two things. The first is to

THINK

about who you really are and what you really want to do with the rest of your life, because if you do something you love, you will be much happier and more likely to be successful than others who are not. However, thinking is one thing; doing is another. Therefore, the second thing I ask each of you to do after you have given some thought to your future is to figure out

HOW

you are going to get to where you want to go. By applying yourself and utilizing the concepts outlined in this book, when it comes time to graduate from college, you could have a substantial competitive advantage over the thousands of other graduates who did little else than go to parties, watch TV, or surf the Internet in their spare time.

When your peers are twenty- or thirty-something and trying to figure out what to do with their lives, you will be on the road to success. There is a good chance you might be their boss. However, the road to success has many bumps and forks in it, and you must remember that *success is a journey, not a destination.* The tools and concepts we have discussed will be able to not only help you today but also help you in the future when you are not certain which fork in the road to take.

As we discussed, each of us has to define what success is for us. But what is the secret to success? At this stage in your life, the younger you can identify your likes and dislikes, start taking responsibility for your future, get focused, and pursue a path that will capitalize on strengths and develop weaknesses to balance your formal and informal learning, the happier you will likely be in your life and chosen career. Don't wait until you are twenty-five to get focused and take responsibility for your future. Start preparing now!

Earlier in this book, we also discussed many factors that may influence your future. That included your friends and family. Remember, while both are important in your life, *you* have to take full responsibility for *your* future. And do not forget about education opportunity costs. Keep your priorities straight and do not become one of those students who has to complete extra semesters or years of study that could have been avoided with proper planning and focus.

Remember that quality employers want to hire quality students. You will be competing for great opportunities against those from your school, city, state, and from across the country. Employers will be putting you against a rating scale, as they have a lot of talent to choose from. Graduating from a postsecondary institution adds points; so do your grades, and so do the relevant skills and experiences you bring.

When I was in college, my father told me that grades were the only thing that mattered, and he judged how smart people were by their grade point average. In reality, grades are only one essential element for future success, and there are other elements that factor in to how intelligent someone is. It can be summed up with another formula which looks something like this:

INTELLIGENCE
=
Book Smarts
+
Street Smarts
+
People Smarts

Being able to read the expression on someone's face or being able to listen to someone's voice and knowing if they are telling the truth are not things you can learn from books. You learn this from life and the interaction with others. When you get into the workforce, you will not have a textbook on your desk. Your formal learning will help with your hard skills, but the soft skills you developed from your informal learning will be a huge key to your progress. This leads me to one more formula, the formula for success. It looks like this:

$$SUCCESS$$
$$=$$
$$Intelligence$$
$$+$$
$$Organizational\ Skills$$
$$+$$
$$Interpersonal\ Skills$$

The better the levels of your book, street, and people smarts, combined with your ability to stay organized and your ability to communicate and influence others, the greater the levels of success you will likely achieve. As you progress on your journey, as it relates to the goals you set for yourself, keeping asking yourself one question: How badly do I want it?

If you want the great opportunities, and there are many of them out there, you can get them. Figure out what you are passionate about, set goals, stay focused, take initiative, apply yourself, and before you know it, you will be the one others are calling "lucky." But what is luck? Luck is what happens when preparation meets opportunity. If I could grow up in a dysfunctional, single-parent family, pay my own way through college, and work for some very well-respected organizations, then guess what? So can you!

I have shared many pieces of personal advice with you, but before I close this book I want to share some pieces of advice from people I met while in college and in the workforce. These pieces of advice have proven to be priceless. They are:

- Pursue life with one goal, and that is to never be ninety years old, reflecting on your life, and starting a sentence with "Gee, I wish I had . . ." Work hard and play hard. In the end, you will regret the things you did not do more than the things you did.

- Life is all about choices. When it comes to making choices, evaluate your options, trust your instincts, and make what you think is the best decision. Do your best and don't look back!
- Whatever you choose to do, do it so well that you set the gold standard. Your work should be how all others are judged.
- Experience is something you do not get until just after you need it. There is no such thing as a bad experience in life, because regardless of what happens, there is a lesson to be learned. Remember: That which does not kill you makes you stronger.
- Life is not always fair. You must take full responsibility for every aspect of your life. It is easy to blame others, but that will only make you angry. If you are that angry, stop talking and do something positive to change the situation.
- Be careful of what you say to whom, especially if it is a negative comment about someone else. You never know who knows whom. If you have something to say, say it to a person's face before you say something behind his or her back. When in doubt, take the high road and keep your mouth shut.

These pieces of advice were shared by people I really respected. I have tried to live by their advice as best as I can, and guess what? It really is good advice to live by.

I also want to share two poems with you. I cannot say that I was a big fan of poetry when I was in high school. But when I got to college and was going through a tough time personally (my grades were falling and I had broken up with my high school sweetheart), I came across the first poem hanging on a plaque in my mother's apartment. The second poem I came across when I was contemplating a year off from college to work instead of getting a student loan, because I did not want to have any debt upon graduation. (I ended up getting the loan.)

I cannot tell you how many times reading these have helped me, and I would be remiss if I did not share them with you. They apply to males and females alike, although one is not written that way. Please do not take offense. I don't know who wrote either of them, as both poems were ascribed as "Author Unknown." If you hit a few bumps in the road over the next few years, for what it is worth, you have my permission to make a copy of these great poems and keep them handy.

The Person Who Thinks He Can

If you think you are beaten, you are;
If you think you dare not, you don't!
If you'd like to win, but you think you can't,
It's almost a cinch that you won't.

If you think you'll lose, you're lost;
For out in the world we find
Success begins with a fellow's will;
It's all in the state of mind!

If you think you're outclassed you are;
You've got to think high to rise.
You've got to be sure of yourself
Before you can win the prize.

Life's battles don't always go
To the strongest or fastest man;
But sooner or later the person who wins
Is the person who thinks he can!

—Author Unknown

Don't Quit

When things go wrong, as they sometimes will;
When the road you're trudging seems all uphill;
When the funds are low; and the debts are high;
And you want to smile, but you have to sigh;
When care is pressing you down a bit—
Rest if you must, but don't you quit.
Success is failure turned inside out;
The silver tint of the clouds of doubt;
And you never can tell how close you are;
It may be near when it seems afar.
So, stick to the fight when you are hardest hit;
It is when things go wrong that you mustn't quit.

—Author Unknown

I want to take this opportunity to thank you for reading this book and to wish you the best for success in your future endeavors! Feel free to drop me a line or send me an e-mail with any questions and to update me on your progress. You can find my full particulars in the about the author section. I'll do my best to answer. Good luck!

Appendix: Graduating Resumé

CURRICULUM VITAE
John R. Jell

Bates Residence #409
McMaster University
Hamilton, Ontario
L8S 4LM
(416) 555-1212

EDUCATION

Bachelor of Commerce   Major: Marketing   1983–1987
McMaster University   Minor: Personnel

Honours Secondary School   North Park Collegiate   1979–1983
Graduation Diploma   Brantford, Ontario

Ontario Scholar in 1983

COCURRICULAR ACTIVITIES (Senior year only with full-time course load)

Senator for the Faculty of Business: Undergraduate representative elected to the university's chief governing body for two-year term.

President of the McMaster Marketing Association: 8-member executive and largest student business club with 500+ members. Led it to its most successful year ever.

Chairman of the Marketing Advisory Council: 10-member executive, geared to special projects and assisting charitable causes.

Vice Chairman of the McMaster Commerce Clubs Council: the governing body for business clubs on campus.

Undergraduate Student Representative on the Faculty of Business Advisory Council: composed of faculty, community, and business leaders

Student Representative Assembly: Exofficio member on the chief student governing body.

Vice President and Cofounder, the McMaster Cycling Association: student group geared to promoting cycling.

General Manager of the McMaster Games Room: the student campus amusement center with responsibility for ten employees. Led it to its most profitable year ever.

Eight committees associated with the above responsibilities are not highlighted.

Previous extracurricular activities will be highlighted upon request.

OTHER AWARDS AND ACTIVITIES

• participated and completed the McMaster Student Union Leadership Skills Seminar in 1986.
• coach of a Minor Pee-Wee hockey team (eleven-year-olds) in 1982–1983.
• chosen to represent my hometown at the "Adventure in Citizenship" Conference in 1982. This conference unites youth from across Canada annually in our nation's capital to get exposure to the workings of the Canadian political and economic systems as well as promote goodwill.
• chosen to participate in a co-op youth employment program in my hometown of Brantford in 1981.
• Honor Society achieved in grades 9, 11, and 12.
• active in helping the campaigns of several local politicians.

WORK EXPERIENCE

General Manager: Sept. 1986–April 1987
  McMaster Games Room
Responsible for the hiring and scheduling of ten employees as well as promoting events on campus and overseeing daily operations of this seven-day-a-week student amusement center. Led the center to its most profitable year ever.

Distribution Representative: May 1986–Sept. 1986
  Coca-Cola Bottling
Assisted in the sales and distribution of Coca-Cola products in the Golden Horseshoe region.

Direct Sales Representative: July 1985–August 1985
  Built-In Vacuum Systems
Sold built-in vacuum cleaner systems to residential homes. My superiors were impressed with my results and offered me my own franchise; however, I declined, in order to complete my education.

Market Research Assistant: August 1985–Sept. 1985
  Agnew Surpass Shoes
Assisted in the compilation of data from a national survey to help the organization determine potential areas to build new stores and increase customer satisfaction.

Retail Sales Representative: August 1985–Sept. 1985
  Black's Camera's
Assisted customers with their photographic needs, whether it was photo-finishing or the purchase of photographic equipment.

Promotional Sales Representative: July 1984–September 1984
  Lynden Park Mall

Responsible for putting a thematic promotion to draw patrons into the mall. I organized and coordinated a sporting goods show by renting mall floor space to local dealers and publicizing the event.

Note: I have also operated my own painting business and worked in the restaurant, newspaper, maintenance, construction, and agriculture industries.

Index

About the Author

John R. Jell was born in Brantford, Ontario, in Canada and raised in a dysfunctional, single-parent family. By the time he turned seventeen, he had to deal with such issues as mental and physical abuse, mental illness, attempted suicide, and alcoholism.

The age of seventeen was a turning point for John. He laid out some plans for his future, which included going to college. He paid his own way through college and earned degrees in business and political science from McMaster University, one of Canada's top universities. While in college, John was frustrated that books did not teach enough real-world skills, so he embarked on a path to develop these skills while maintaining a full-time course load.

Based on his preparation, upon graduating from college he was immediately hired by The Coca-Cola Company, which created a position for him. At the time, Coca-Cola was one of the hottest companies on the planet and did not recruit from colleges in his area. The company preferred to hire people with three to five years of professional experience gained at another company's expense.

John began his career with Coca-Cola as a sales supervisor at the age of twenty-two, the youngest in Canada at the time. At twenty-five he was promoted to assistant sales manager, the youngest in Canada at the time. Two years later he was promoted to logistics analyst, and at twenty-eight he became the national manager of distribution development. At twenty-nine he became the first person ever promoted from the bottling company in Canada to the parent company in the United States. At the time of assuming the position of cold-drink development manager in Los Angeles, he was the youngest individual (by fourteen years to his closest peer) in that position in the United States and was responsible for developing one of Coca-Cola's most lucrative business segments, which represented over $350 million in sales. At the age of thirty-four, he was recruited by Weisman Enterprises, one of North America's largest transaction management companies, to be its vice president of sales for the western United States and Canada. Keeping with tradition, Mr. Jell was its youngest vice president when hired. Today, John is employed by the world's #1 food company, Nestlé, where he oversees beverage strategic channel new business development for Nestlé USA-Foodservices.

John's passions for writing this book, and his original "advanced" version, began while in college. After graduating, he was invited to speak to the freshman body at his college on preparing for life after school. Realizing the need for a student-friendly book on the topic, over a period of ten years he worked with many educators, students, and business professionals to fine-tune the content of his books prior to publication. The endorsements on the cover were a result.

Because of his message and motivating speaking style, numerous national, state, regional, and local educational organizations have asked John to do keynote addresses and workshops at major conferences. Some of these groups include:

- American Vocational Association (now ACTE)
- Future Business Leaders of America
- National Curriculum Integration Conference
- State of Missouri Department of Education
- State of North Carolina Department of Public Instruction
- State of Mississippi Department of Education
- State of California Youth Volunteer Corps.

John is a sought-after motivational speaker. He serves as a school-to-career expert on numerous websites. Having been one himself, John Jell also works with at-risk youth.

If you would like Mr. Jell to speak at an upcoming event, autograph your book, or answer a question, please write or e-mail:

John R. Jell
JELL Corporation
P.O. Box 55543
Sherman Oaks, CA 91413-5543
(818) 986-3004
E-mail: john@johnjell.com